CEREMONIES

of the

INDIGENOUS & NATIVE

AMERICAN ASSOCIATION OF

NATIONS

Published by RaMus Publications in Association with Indigenous Education. Indedu.org
Original Copyright ©2020 All rights reserved under International and Indigenous Laws and Conventions and United States
INARS catalog number 11062003
ISBN: 978-1-7358970-0-4

You may be surprised to find that many of our customs and traditions are remarkably similar to many of the traditional things you do today. That is because we really have the same culture "human", <u>with some different local customs and traditions</u>. Please do not be afraid to <u>add</u> any of these if not all of these ceremonies to your everyday activities, they belong to you.

An example of our culture that you may think is foreign to you but is not is the attention that we pay to our ancestors. Many of us have pictures of loved ones that have passed over. All of us still place these pictures on mantles in our living rooms and on walls in our homes.

In our customs we relate to our ancestors as the heavenly ones, or our heavenly parents because they have left us our traditions, the land, and life itself. A supplication in memory of them would go like this:

"Oh, Heavenly Ones Who Are Our Sustainers, We Do Accept The Duty That You Have Lain On Us to Continue the faith; And To Clean Up The Filth Made By The Non-Submitting Ones".

We see them as sustainers because they gave birth to us and they give us a path to travel; these were and are our heroes, in our traditions.

"The heroes are not individuals who raised up with a history which remained written in the past; the heroes in our tradition were those who gave their life in an effort to reach the objectives of history written as the future by the ancients, <u>building for generations that would follow the steps; and they were dedicated to that history that was forthcoming, the history of the clans and the tribes, dedicated to the future that was already written</u>. Future and history were united with the life to come and with the dead past which was already gone". Lord of the Voice, *Thunderbird Publications in association of INARS*

Similitudes that many of you can identify with are times when you pray or sit in memory of lost relatives, or when remembering old times of long lost friends; or looking at the old pictures that we all enjoy at family outings and gatherings remembering relatives that have crossed over. We make a prayer to The Giver of Breath to protect us as he did our ancestors. To the Great Spirit Giver of Breath, we say:

"Oh, Our Sustainer (Giver of Breath) We Beseech You, To Keep Your Hand Over Us, To Control the Strings of The Courses of Our Lives; Our Sustainer, And If We Do Wrong or Make a Mistake, Please Shower Your Divine Blessings And Forgiveness On Us, You Are The Only One That Can Raise Us As True Followers Of Truth, And In Your Name We Will Always Carry On."

We have supplied you with a number of MBC/INAAN ceremonies in this small book:

· Two naming ceremonies,

·A birthing ceremony,

·Two coming of age ceremonies,

·Two marriage ceremony,

·The dedicating ceremony for land, the home etc.,

·The Fire Ceremony,

·The death and burial ceremony,

The marriage ceremony takes you on a journey through time. At different points in this ceremony the bride, groom and the assembly are taken through a pageant of some marriage ceremonial experiences of our people at different periods in our story in America.

The supplications and prayers are simply sayings of the masters of each of major religions, all of them. We make no distinction as to an individuals' faith.

One of the objectives of this work is to inform you of our historical culture; another is to assist you with combining the old with the new.

In our publications we have placed information from thousands of years ago about our ancient Guale/Yamassee connections from various locations from Northern to Southern West Africa, and about others from around the globe. For more information see Proto Guale/Yamassee "Revised Edition"

Burning of Incense and Smudging with Sacred Herbs

The burning of incense and or smudging have been common practice amongst our people in every culture that we have lived and learned about.

The use of incense and or smudging each person in a group, circle, ceremony, or the venue, is a custom we will continue to use. Starting from the East and holding incense or the smudge pot lit in the venue, each person can bathe themselves in the smoke, or smudge the head, heart, arms, then down the body and down the legs. You can choose to smudge or just bathe in the smoke of the incense of oils.

The burning of incense and smudging with sacred herbs brings us positive energy and helps us to communicate with the Giver of Breath.

Smudge the room, slowly walking clockwise following the path of the Wheel of Life around the room, fanning the incense or smudge pot, keeping it lit fanning the smoke.

On the traditional Guale/Yamassee Native American wheel of life, life begins on the square, at 90º degrees, and in the East. The teenage years are in the South, 180º, 270º is mid-life in the West, 360º is in the north, by this time we are elders and nearly ready for the "Etheric World". Yet the journey is not over, we go to the Etheric World for the next parts in the cycle. The wheel teaches balance, harmony and the brotherhood of man.

The MBC, Guale/Yamassee Wheel of Life

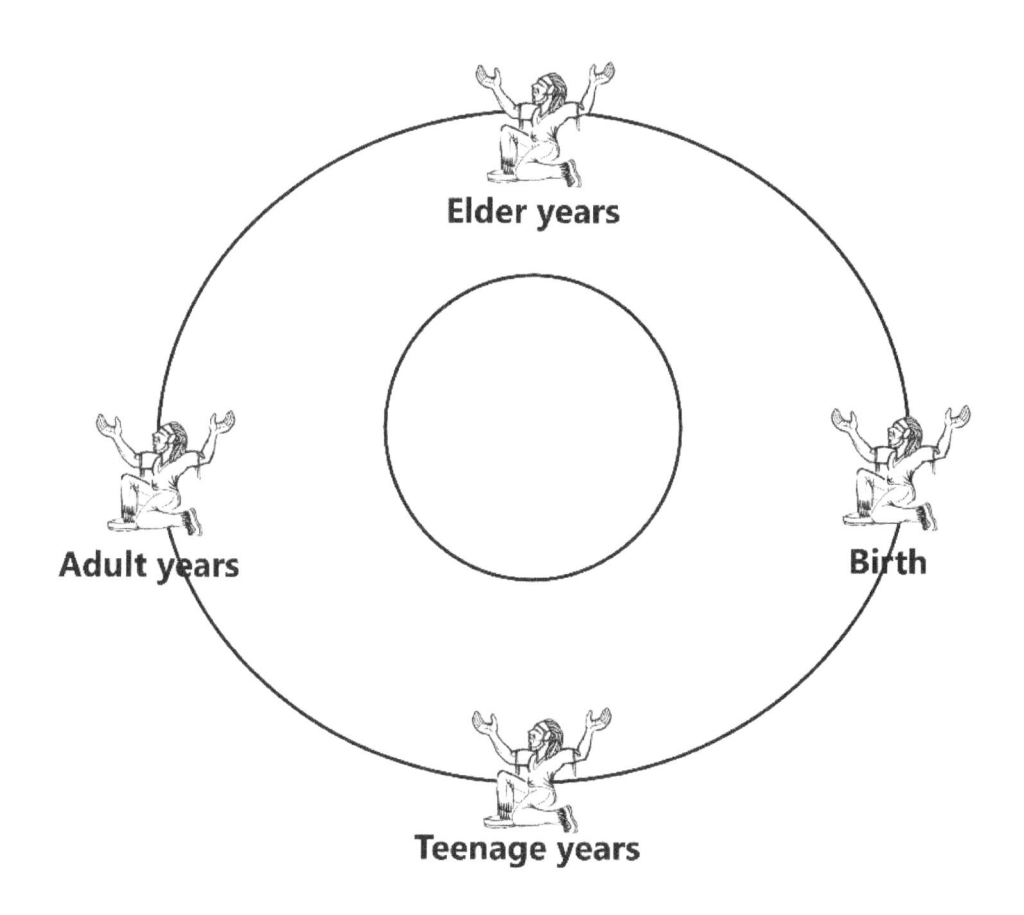

Elder years

Adult years

Birth

Teenage years

We write for the education of the MBC/INAAN peoples.

The book is prepared in Gualean Yamassic and in English. This is done for non- Gualean-Yamassic speakers to aide in teaching the cultural ethic, and the language. Some of the selections are translated word for word. I hope that this will be of assistance to you. Some of the thoughts are not translated. Try translating them, you may find it fun and educational.

The beginning of the book we have complete ceremonies. The second part of the book is prayers, thoughts, and other remembrances we share as indigenous peoples. I hope you will enjoy them.

Our literature is written to teach us MBC/INAAN peoples; not to blame or cast a shade upon any race or clan of peoples. As I said in my last book, all of us had a hand in slavery; the Europeans were just a little more systematically brutal, and Jim Crow was one of their crown jewels. Well, I guess Jim Crow was quite shady.

Do not use the information to beat down others. This information is not for them. They may read if they wish. There will be no cry for recruitment. This is for you, "MBC/INAAN" nationals, and your families.

MBC/INAAN is neither a club nor a fraternity. MBC/INAAN is not an order, nor a church. As individuals, we may belong to any of the above type organizations as this is a matter of personal self-determination which all man has a right to.

"Mund Bareefan Gabelu/Clan" of House Thunderbird, is an indigenous tribe/family. "MBC" is the maker/establisher, and custodian of the Indigenous Native American Government named INAAN.

To the peoples of the Yamasee Union of Eatonton Georgia, Mund Bareefan Gabelu Indigenous Native American Association of Nations is the chosen government of Grand Chief Black Thunderbird Eagle as his indigenous government in America; and as the indigenous representative for the clans, tribes, and indigenous peoples of the Yamassee Union of 1997 which was under his leadership and authority.

Istagwaad - Introduction

First, we give gratitude to The Giver of Breath, and the heavenly ones for guiding us with preparing this book.

I am Black-Hawk Thunderbird, Most Principal Chief, of Mund Bareefan Clan. We are Guale/Yamassee Native Americans. We are indigenous

My effort is to lead us into our rightful place in the international world and to restore our Native American culture. I am the Authenticator; I have authenticated our presence as indigenous people(s) of America and in the international world. When? On February 11th, 2004. We <u>are in our time</u>.

We would like to thank everyone that helped us with this work. Special thanks to Naasiyra Love El, for all her help on this project. <u>Thank you Naasiyra</u>.

To all "INAAN" nationals: Now is the time. We can't wait any longer. Come and take the next the step amongst other indigenous people of the planet as who we are, were, and who we shall be known as hence forth. We are "Tribal, Indigenous, Original Americans".

This book is a book of some culture and customs of the (MBC/INAAN). This is "**Not THE Book**" of Customs, **it's a** book of some of our culture and customs.

Once again, many of you all were helpful to us with preparing this book. We thank you all. Thanks, and thanks to the Giver of Breath, for giving us the strength to carry on.

I have inserted ancient Guale/Yamassee customs into this book along with some others that are not as old, and some that are new.

This book is prepared for your education. Read it. Study it. Make it a part of your lives, and through it, the Giver of Breath will guide you all through life. If we teach our story and customs to our children, they will keep our customs in their hearts, and they will teach these and other "INAAN" customs to their children.

"We advocate this...

That which is the essence of Humans is fashioned in the image and the likeness of the INVISIBLE Giver of Breath, born before all living things.

That means you are a part of that which created the terrestrial and celestial Universe, you are a part of the visible thing and the invisible thing.

It means that the Spirit Giver of Breath is the pattern or beginning;

and the end or completion of the Created Universe. "The One" is before everything and the Universe has in it, its consistency.

The Great Spirit of the Creative Forces of the Galactic Universes is present in the Universe from its origin.

In consequence, the distinction does not settle down "between spirit and nature, but among the different grades of realization, and the principle "SPIRIT in Human Beings" and SPIRIT in Nature

Lord of the Voice

Part 1

Ceremonies of

MBC/INAAN

A FIRE CEREMONY

A FIRE CEREMONY

WHAT IS A FIRE CEREMONY?

The **fire ceremony** is a Native American practice that is performed during the full moon but, you do not have to wait for a full moon to do a fire ceremony. Fire Ceremonies are wonderful during a New Moon, and at any time during or in conjunction with other ceremonies like at the solstices and equinoxes. This Native American ceremony is a grand ceremony, but it is easy. Most commonly the fire ceremony is done at the point of the Full and New Moons.

HOW IS A FIRE CEREMONY PERFORMED?

During the full moon each of us may bring something to burn that we would like to free from our past and/or a pray asking for something new that we will also burn, turning them into smoke traveling within the ethers.

This lets the old desires burn along to its highest spiritual paths, and the new prayer also asking to burn along to its highest spiritual path. We can bring pictures, drawings and intentions written on paper to the past or to the newness.

We form a circle around the fire and one by one we call for help from Giver of Breath. We begin with a prayer and end with a prayer that is shared with gratitude that our prayers and desires will rid the unfortunate deeds and bring in the new.

Here is a prayer asking for changing the past which is burned and freed within the ethers thereby changing the past.

A Prayer to change the past:

Oh, Heavenly Ones Who Are Our Sustainers, We Do Accept The Duty That You Have Lain upon Us; To Clean Up The Filth Made By The Non-Submitting ones.

The past burned and freed, we then have something prepared that is also written down on clean paper for newness and success for the future.

Then we recite.

Oh, (Hotala Manneyto) our Sustainer We Beseech You, To Keep Your Hand Over Us, To Control The Strings Of The Courses Of Our Lives; Our Sustainer, And If We Do Wrong, Please Shower Your Divine Blessings And Forgiveness On Us, You Are The Only One That Can Raise Us As True Followers Of Truth, And In Your We Will Always Carry On.

Then we make supplication to "Hold On":

A Prayer Hold Old:

Hold on to what is good even if it is a handful of earth. Hold on to your faith even if it is a tree which stands by itself. Hold on to what you must do even if it is a long way from here. Hold on to life even when it is easier letting go. Hold on to my hand even when I have gone away from you."

Remember, what you have written on clean paper and placed into the fire which has burned to smoke and ash, is to remove the old desire; and to call in the new. The things we address from our past or call to our future can be shared with the group or kept to ourselves as we go through the Fire Ceremony.

Keep in mind; no one is obligated/ordered to speak during the Fire Ceremonies. Anyone can participate without saying what they are letting go or calling forth.

YOU WILL NEED ALL OF THE FOLLOWING:

A fire pit or fireplace where you can safely burn a fire. A barbecue pit or fireproof pot works well too. If you live in an apartment, it is best to find a place outdoors where you can safely burn a fire.

You will need a fire extinguisher, a bucket filled with water, or a water hose to put the fire out after the ceremony.

Items such as a drawing, picture, or written intentions that you would like to release from your past or bring forward should be brought to the fire pit, and/or anything else that you feel would serve your need to be brought forward or released at the pit.

After your fire gets going, each person may contribute to the prayer and then the items are offered to the fire. Tell The Great Spirit and all the Divine Spirits that you have called forth that you offer these things in thanksgiving. Meditate and feel the presence of The Great Spirit all around you. Singing praise, playing peaceful music either through tapes or instruments may also be used.

In strict Native American custom - Sage, tobacco or sweetgrass is burned along with the past and with our intentions towards the future. When the smoke rises up into the ethers our intentions are carried away to The Creative Forces of the Universe.

There should be a quiet or meditative break in order to embrace a new awareness of transformation in your life. It is also symbolic that you can offer up a bit of food you wanted and only ate half of, that you could offer the other half in thanks.

A TIME FOR CELEBRATION

You can sing, dance, and enjoy yourself. Experience a feeling of thanksgiving that your prayers are already answered. This is a time of celebration. Every Divine Source you called in is present, so give thanks and believe you have already received.

A MOST IMPORTANT QUOTE

"Therefore, I say unto you; what things so ever you desire, when you pray, believe that ye receive them, and you shall have them."

Mark 11:2

The Short Naming Ceremony

The Short Naming Ceremony

Oh, Our Guardians, There Is No Openers Except You-all. All Our Gratitude Is For You-all. We Are Your Offspring, And We Ask You For Help. Please Guide Us And Our Children To The Way Of The Ones, Who Are In Truth. The Way Of Those Who You Have Bestowed Your Grace; Not Those Who Have Been Cursed, Nor Of Those Who Have Gone Astray From Truth.

Have you taken a name?

Yes, my name is.

_____.

Official "I bring _____ and _____, to our ancestors, to our Heavenly Guardians, and to our Clan, we pray that this man/woman will always walk in the grace of All."

The Affirmation

I am in the love of All, and all love is me I am a part of All and All is a part of me. I am one with All and All is one with me. I can succeed as a part of All and fail as an individual. I can be all that

25

I wish in All, as long as my wish is to stay in All. I am never alone. All is, I am, All can, I can, All does, I do.

Birth and Presentation Ceremony

Birth and Presentation Ceremony

Smudge the birthing room if possible. Slowly walk clockwise following the path of the Guale/Yamassee wheel of life around the room, fanning the incense or smudge pot, keep it lit, and fan the smoke. If you cannot smudge the venue, be sure to attempt to smudge the representative(s) of the mother, the following supplication should be recited at least 9 times during the birth……

Note: It has been our custom and shall be to take the placenta to a spot chosen by the family or by the clan for burial plots; or in approved private burial plots; sweeten it with honey or dates and to bury the placenta deeply about two feet into the ground in a bio-degradable container with the placenta uncovered inside the bio-degradable container.

Oh, Our Guardians There Is No Opener Except You-all. All Our Gratitude Is For You-all. We Are Your Offspring, And We Ask You For Help. Please Guide Us And Our Children To The Way Of The Ones, Who Are In Truth. The Way Of Those On Who You Have Bestowed Your Grace; Not Those Who Have Been Cursed, Nor Of Those Who Have Gone Astray From Truth.

The Grand Naming Ceremony

The Grand Naming Ceremony

"A good name is to be chosen rather than great riches, loving favor rather than silver and gold." From Sayud Solomon

It is important that our children are given names that have strong Native American themes. We should give them names that they can live up to or strive to become.

Presentation Ceremony

This ceremony is designed to be performed by both parents.

Please remember that our children are learning from day one, there is no tomorrow for them. Every day is now teaching them love, honor, to respect others and themselves. Children will emulate everything they see, so make each moment positive for them. Make sure all your actions are things you want them to see and/or hear, for they are always watching. In children we have a beautiful gift. We have the future of our nation in them.

Actual ceremony proceedings:

Maku read out loud as the family is approaching:

"A good name is rather to be chosen than great riches, and loving favor rather-than silver or gold". Sayud Solomon

Supplication Three

Glory Be To My Sustainers Glory Be To The Heavenly Ones, Sustainers, Possessors Of Majesty. Glory Be To My Heavenly Parents. Glory Be To You, Oh Heavenly Ones. No Mortals Would Exist As Humans If You Didn't Appoint And Conceive Us.

Mother Recite: "Oh Giver of Breath and all good energy/sprits, make him/her dutiful and one who trembles at the mention of Anu and bring him up in to his/her full growth"

Official Recite "Oh Great Spirit and All His Heavenly Beings, Bestow Your Knowledge Of The Old Ways On Him, And Give Him/her The Wisdom And The Faith."

Father Recite: "Oh Giver of Breath and All His Spiritual Beings, I Commend her/him and hers/his offspring into your protection from All Evil".

Official Recite: "I Seek Refuge In The Giver of Breath 's Perfect Words, From The Evil Of Every Evil, And From The Evil Of Every Malicious Eye of the evil spirit.

Father will now take the baby and raise him or her before the clan to the heavens and declare: "(Child's name),

---

Both parents recite Supplication 27 – There Is No Opener Except The Guardians:

Supplication Twenty-seven
Oh, Our Guardians, There Is No Openers Except You-all. All Our Gratitude Is For You-all. We Are Your Offspring, And We Ask You For Help. Please Guide Us And Our Children To The Way Of The Ones, Who Are In Truth. The

Way Of Those Who You Have Bestowed Your Grace; Not Those Who Have Been Cursed, Nor Of Those Who Have Gone Astray From Truth.

After this recitation, the parents hand the child to each generation in his family (Example: Grandfathers, Grandmothers, Uncles, Aunts, Child's Older Brothers and Sisters and then back to Parents)

When the child is returned to parents, they will present the child to the Clan:

"We, the _____ family, present our child(ren) _____to our ancestors, to Our Heavenly Guardians, and to our Clan, we pray that this child(ren) will always walk in the grace of All." Amun

Ceremony is ended after everyone recites an Affirmation.

A Family Prayer

The Creative forces of the universe made us a family

We need one another

We love one another

We forgive one another

We work together

We play together

We worship together

Together we use guidance from the ancient ones

Together we grow in memory of our ancestors

Together we love all humans

Together we serve The Giver of Breath

Together we build for paradise

These are our hopes and thoughts

Help us to attain them, O Giver of Breath,

In our names and the names of Our Ancestors.

This can be trusted.

At this time, the infant child is returned to his or her mother. Child is not to be handled by people outside of the family until mother approves it, usually around three (3) months or more.

Clan

Coming of Age Ceremony

Clan Daughters
Coming of Age Ceremony

A ritual ceremony being performed during the time when our daughters become young women is probably as old as time itself. Yet somewhere along the timeline, we got caught up in another people's way of life, and the woman's monthly cycle became something to be ashamed of, something never to be spoken about – it became a curse. Nothing is further from the truth – this is nature's way of letting each young woman know that she is a mother to this planet, she is a hope of our future. This ceremony can be celebrated any time after a young woman has had three (3) consecutive menses.

This is a sacred time! Sisters may grumble and disagree but if they are honest – the truth is there. Women have the power to make or break a man. Women have the power to make or break their children. So, it is only common sense to realize that women have the power to make or break our nation. This coming of age ceremony is an opportunity to include all members of our clan in the restoration of our sacred rituals.

To the elders, each of you has special attributes that are needed for our Clan Daughters to flourish and grow. They need your support the same way seedlings need to be cared for – they need to be protected, so that they will be an asset to our nation, and to others. There is a contract signing between Father, Mother and Clan Daughter each member confirming that the daughter will learn the following with an above average capability, in addition to her regular class studies: Keeping of Our Sacred Rituals, Family Guide Parenting Classes, Indigenous Studies, MBC/INAAN Constitution, Home Economics, (with stress on finances, money management), entrepreneurship, Drivers Education, Herbology and Excess to Vocational Trades. The contract is then witnessed by at least three Matrons.

Recommended at Home Preparations:

Prior to coming to ceremony, daughters will have started to fast upon waking (fasting will end during ceremony under the direction of An Official) ** Intake of clear fluids or water or fruit is allowed**. Daughters are to make major ablution (instruction should be from mother or older female member of family). NO ALCOHOL PERFUMES ONLY PURE BODY OILS SHOULD BE USED. This is a time of meditation and mother/daughter bonding (question and answer time, chanting, and helping daughter dress and do hair).

Actual ceremony proceedings:

There is one gold circle, which represents the four directions, and 360 degrees of knowledge. There will be a gold walkway (which extends like a ray) for each girl participating in the ceremony. The walkway represents the straight path on which each of us strives to walk and stay on. At the entrance of the walkway is an arch, which represents the womb, the nurturer of life. This arch is decorated with flowers (the color of the four elements) and fruit (which represent the abundance of life).

Green leaves, which represent land (ARD).

Blue flowers, which represent water (MOYA).

Yellow flowers, which represent air (HAWU).

Red flowers, which represent fire (NA,UR).

There is a pathway as the family enters the room or area, just pass where they will be greeted by a Clan Chief, there are two long white candles that are for each parent's lineage. One candle is to be lit by the father and the other by the mother. The Clan Daughter (representing the 5th element) garbed in an ankle length purple dress or robe (purple represents our royal seed, our Creative Force of Will) will enter room on the right arm of her father, older brother, or male guardian with her mother or female guardian accompanying on the left.

Father shall walk mother and daughter to the presiding Chief who asks the following:
Chief- "Who brings forth this daughter to our clan?"
Parents: I, _____, and I, _____, present our daughter ____, to the Clan for guidance and protection.
The Clan Chief then directs them on to be received by a Clan Matron. They proceed forward, light the white ancestral candles, and wait to be addressed by the Grand Matron. (Both father and mother light a white candle in honor of both of the family lines.)

Chief-"Train up a child in the way he should go and when he is old, he will not depart from it.   Master Solomon

The Grand Matron asks, "Why do you bring your daughter to me"?

Mother responds: Our daughter _____ has become a woman by the laws of nature."

Father responds: "My daughter comes with much to learn; she comes here willingly to learn the duties of our clan."

Matron addresses daughter: "Daughter speak to your ancestors."

Matron then asks daughter: "Daughter what are ten virtues of a Good Woman?"

Daughter will respond:

1. It is a must that she is always clean and smelling good.

2. It is a must that she is always pleasant.

3. It is a must that she has a noble character, that she can be respected and obeyed.

4. It is a must that she is loyal to her husband and disciplines herself in order to keep a respectful relationship.

5. It is a must that her home is a place of harmony and peace for her family and that all guests are made to feel welcome.

6. It is a must that she sets an example and be a role model for her children. By the example of her nature, grace and deeds, her daughters will want to emulate her, and her sons will have a role model for which to choose their wives.

7. It is a must that she maintains honesty and integrity.

8. It is a must that she controls her emotions and to be strong under pressure and always keeps her promises.

9. It is a must that she be an asset to her family and her clan.

10. It is a must that she be a mother to all children and a daughter to all elders within her clan.

Grand Matron addresses daughter: "Daughter if you are willing to accept your duties towards your family and clan enter through the arch and walk the path. Walk the circle in honor of our ancestors twice symbolic of 720 degrees of knowledge (as above so below), then return down the path to the Clan."

As the daughter enters the arch, the Clan will recite together the following as one voice,

Supplication- Prayer of the Aiders:

Oh, Heavenly Ones Who Are Our Sustainers, We Do Accept The Duty That You Have Lain Upon Us; To Recover From The Trials of Our Past…

Oh (Giver of Breath) Our Sustainer We Beseech You, To Keep Your Hand Over Us, To Control The Strings Of The Courses Of Our Lives; Our Sustainer, And If We Do Wrong, Please Shower Your Divine Blessings And Forgiveness On Us, You Are The Only One That Can Raise Us As True Followers Of Truth, And In Your Name We Will Always Carry On. and

Supplication- **About The Source:**

In My Quest To Be A Being, That Is One With You In Perfection And Love, I Come To The Source "The Giver of

Breath, And Greet Them With A True And Loving Heart, And I Know that He Love Me.

He Is The One That Has United Us With All Of You, The Supreme Spirits. The Best One, Oh Guardians, Those Who Form The Circle Of The Master-The Spirit Of Guidance,

We Are One Unit; We are In All. All Is Us; All Is Going To Help Us. All Loves Us. We Are One With You. Oh, Ancients, Elders, Accept Us, Accept Us Amun. Oh, Ancients, Elders, Accept Us, Accept Us Amun.   Traditional

As the young women exit at the arch from within the circle, she acknowledges who she is.

I am _____, daughter of _____ and _____ , and I will l follow in the footsteps of my mother and my father and bear the banner of the True Aiders of The Giver of Breath. She then shall recite the supplication "A Family Prayer" to the clan.

Ceremony is ended after everyone recites

A Family Prayer

The Creative forces of the universe made us a family.

We need one another. We love one another.

We forgive one another. We work together.

We play together We worship together.

Together we use guidance from the ancient ones.

Together we grow in memory of our ancestors.

Together we love all humans.

Together we serve The Giver of Breath.

Together we build for paradise.

These are our hopes and thoughts.

Help us to attain them, O Giver of Breath,

In our names and the names of Our Ancestors This can be trusted.

Young Man's Coming of Age Ceremony

Young Man's Coming of Age Ceremony

This ceremony can be celebrated after the 13th birthday. The ceremony should be performed in a purple circle. If this is not possible, family and friends should form a circle.

There are four candles, which represent the four elements which are placed in the circle. The candles are placed inside the circle in the shape of a square to make four corners inside of the circle:

One candle is green, which represents land (ARD).

One candle is blue, which represents water (MOYA).

One candle is yellow, which represents air (HAWU).

One candle is red, which represents fire (NA'UR).

The Young Man, representing the 5th element, will stand inside the purple circle. Purple represents our royal seed, our Creative Force of Will. Four candles are placed inside the circle representing a square. These two shapes represent the 720 degrees of knowledge that Masters hold.

Each shape individually represents 360 degrees of knowledge that we strive to obtain. The proceedings begin with the young man standing in the center of these two geometric shapes.

There is a contract signing between Father, Son and Clan Chief that declares that the Young Man should fulfill the following in addition to regular class studies within a five year time frame:

General Education, Customs Books, Family Guide, Indigenous Studies, MBC/INAAN Constitution Home Economics (stress on money management and entrepreneurship), Driver Education, Agriculture, (including the operation of heavy equipment), Herb-ology, Outdoor Survival Training, Vocational Trade, Carpentry, Parenting Classes...

Actual ceremony proceedings:

As the participants step up to the Chief, the chief will proclaim:

Chief- "Train up a child in the way he should go, and when he is old,   he will not depart from it."   Master Solomon

Chief, read Supplication:

My Quest

In My Quest To Be A Being, That Is One With You In Perfection And Love, I Come To The Source "The Giver of Breath And We Greet Him With a Loving Heart.

And I Thank You For House Royal Thunderbird, And Greet Them With A True And Loving Heart, And I Know That All The Clan, Stands With Me.

We Are The Ones That Has United With You, The Supreme Spirits. The Best One, Oh Guardians, Those Who Form The Circle Of The Master-The Spirit Of Guidance,

We Are One Unit; We Are In All. All Is Us; All Is Going To Help Us. All Loves Us. We Are One With You. Oh, Ancients, Elders, Accept Us, Accept Us Amun. Oh, Ancients, Elders, Accept Us, Accept Us Amun.   Master B.TH Eagle

The Chief will now say:

It is important for the community to take an active role in the development of our youth.

The Chief will summon the family forward:

Father, Mother And Son Come Forward, Step Within The Circle

Parents Recite Supplication:

No Opener Except You

Oh, My Guardians, There Is No Opener Except You. All My Gratitude Is For You. I Am Your Offspring, And I Ask You For Help. Please Guide Me And My Child To The Way Of The Ones, Who Are In Truth. The Way Of Those Who You Have Bestowed Your Grace; Not Those Who Have Been Cursed, Nor Of Those Who Have Gone Astray From Truth.

Mother then recites her own poem or prayer about how she feels about this new stage in her son's life.

Example:

Thirteen years ago, I labored and you _____ were born, I was there for every first in your life, each word, each tooth, each step. I stand here now, proud of you.

My son, as you make this journey on a path where I do not walk, for your path to manhood, your father must now guide you. But I remain always your mother, to support you emotionally and spiritually during your ups and downs,

I step to the side as you spread your wings, father and son, teacher and student. Grow into a good man, one people can respect. Know that your word is your bond. The only thing I ask of you is my goodnight kiss and hug. Live life well. Live as if each day is your last and submit only to The Giver of Breath. .

Mother now walks to the outside of the square and lights four candles with a black candle.

Chief: *"Why do you bring your son to me?"*
Father responds: *"My son comes with much to learn; he comes here willingly to learn the duties of our clan."*

Maku then asks son: *"Son what are ten virtues of a Good Man?"*

Son will respond:

1. It is a must that he is always clean and smelling good.
2. It is a must that he is always pleasant.
3. It is a must that he has a noble character, that he can be respected and obeyed.
4. It is a must that he is loyal to his mate or mates and disciplines himself in order to keep respectful relationships.
5. It is a must that his home is a place of harmony and peace for his family and that all guests are made to feel welcome.
6. It is a must that he sets an example and be a role model for his children. By the example of his nature, grace and deeds, his sons will want to emulate him, and his daughters will have a role model for which to choose their husbands.
7. It is a must that he maintains honesty and integrity.
8. It is a must that he controls his emotions and to be strong

under pressure and always keeps his promises.

9. It is a must that he be an asset to his family and his clan.

10. It is a must that he be a father to all children and a son to all elders within his clan

Father addresses son: *"Son, if you are willing to accept your duties towards your family and clan, walk the circle with me, in honor of our ancestors twice, symbolic of 720 degrees of knowledge."* (as above so below).

As the son and father walk the circle, the Clan will recite together the following as one voice,

Supplication **Prayers of the Aiders**

Oh, Heavenly Ones Who Are Our Sustainers, We Do Accept The Duty That You Have Lain Upon Us; To Recover From The Trials of Our Past... Oh (Giver of Breath) Our Sustainer We Beseech You, To Keep Your Hand Over Us, To Control The Strings Of The Courses Of Our Lives; Our Sustainer, And If We Do Wrong, Please Shower Your Divine Blessings And Forgiveness On Us, You Are The Only One That Can Raise Us

As True Followers Of Truth, And In Your Name We Will Always Carry On.

About The Source

In My Quest To Be A Being, That Is One With You In Perfection And Love, I Come To The Source "The Giver of Breath, And Greet Them With A True And Loving Heart, And I Know that He Loves Me. He Is The One That Has United Us With All Of You, The Supreme Spirits. The Best One, Oh Guardians, Those Who Form The Circle Of The Master-The Spirit Of Guidance, We Are One Unit; We are In All. All Is Us; All Is Going To Help Us. All Loves Us. We Are One With You. Oh, Ancients, Elders, Accept Us, Accept Us Amun. Oh, Ancients, Elders, Accept Us, Accept Us Amun.

Traditional

The Young Man from within the circle, acknowledges who he is:

I am _____, son of _____ and _____ , and I shall follow in the footsteps of my mother and my father and bear the banner of the True Aiders of .The Giver of Breath.

Young Man then reads Supplication **I Have Trust**

I Have Trust In You, Oh Heavenly Sprits and I Am Content With You As My Sustainers, And I Am Content With Hagug As My Way Of Life And I Am Content With Your Chosen Ones, Please Make Me One Of The Best Of Your Humble Children. Accept My Appreciation Of the House "Royal Thunderbird", For Opening My Eyes To Truth. For Lifting The Spell Of Ignorance, That Has Been Laid On Your Children For Thousands Of Years. I Am Ever So Grateful For Having Become Guale/Yamassee. It Has Changed My Life Forever, And Now I Know My Way Home To You. I Am No Longer One Of Those Who Are Ignorant To You.

And then he reads supplication **Prayer of the Aiders**

Oh, Heavenly Ones Who Are Our Sustainers, We Do Accept The Duty That You Have Lain upon Us; To Clean Up The Filth Made By The Non-Submitting ones.

Oh (Giver of Breath) our Sustainer We Beseech You, To Keep Your Hand Over Us, To Control The Strings Of The Courses Of Our Lives; Our Sustainer, And If We Do Wrong, Please Shower Your Divine Blessings And Forgiveness On Us, You Are The Only One That Can Raise Us As True Followers Of Truth, And In Your Name We Will Always Carry On.

Father shall come forward and recites his poem or prayer expressing his feelings and future obligations to his son. (Optional)

The ceremony will close by reciting **A Family Prayer**

A Family Prayer

The Creative forces of the universe made us a family.

We need one another.

We love one another.

We forgive one another.

We work together.

We play together.

We worship together.

Together we use guidance from the ancient ones.

Together we grow in memory of our ancestors.

Together we love all humans.

Together we serve The Giver of Breath.

Together we build for paradise.

These are our hopes and thoughts.

Help us to attain them, O Giver of Breath.

In our names and the names of Our Ancestors This can be trusted.

The Marriage Ceremony

(The Short Ceremony)

The Marriage Ceremony

The Short Ceremony

Begin with Official reciting the following:

"And He Said Unto Them, Have Ye Not Read, That He Which Made Them At The Beginning Made Them Male And Female, And Said, To This Case Should A Man Leave His Father And Mother And Cleve Unto His Wife: And They Twain Shall l Be One Flesh. Wherefore They Shall l No More Twain, But One Flesh. What Therefore The Great Spirit Has Joined Together Let No One Put Asunder."

Master Matthew

Verse of The Chair

"The Giver of Breath (The Great Spirit) is he; and without Him, nothing would exist, The Living, The Eternal who never tires nor takes a second from His creation, to slumber or to sleep. For Him is whatever is in the Galactic Heavens and in the planet Earth. Who is he, that can intercede with Him except by His permission? He knows what is between their hands (what works their hands do) and what they leave behind; but they cannot comprehend anything from His knowledge except what He pleases. Spread

wide is His Seat in the Galactic Heavens and the planet Earth, and the Guardianship of Both of Them is no burden for Him Because He is the Most High, the Supreme.
Master Mustafa

Vows may be read at this point that are written by the bride and groom.

_____

_____

_____.

The Wrapping of the Hands

Bring together the right hands of the groom and the right hand of the bride. The hands shall be wrapped in a white shawl. If there are rings, the bride and groom shall put the rings on.

Groom... *I stand before The Giver of Breath and declare "Behold, you are consecrated (sacred) Unto Me By This Ring According To The Customs Of MBC/INAAN* .

Bride... *"Blessed art thou Oh Giver of Breath who makes the Bridegroom to rejoice with the Bride."*

Official: *"Oh, Hotala Manney to Make These Loved Companions Greatly Rejoice, Even As You Did Gladden Your Creature In The*

Earth of Old, Blessed are you Oh Our Sustainer Who Makes Bridegroom And Bride Rejoice."

Now In The Presence of This Gathering; and By The Power granted Me By The Giver of Breath , and MBC/INAAN Government, I now pronounce you Husband and Wife.

The Marriage Ceremony

(The Grand Ceremony)

The Marriage Ceremony

(The Grand Ceremony)

The pouring of libations

Drumming and music Of The Hour

Processional

Opening Supplications

Pouring Of Libation

Blessing Of The Elders

Istathbaat (Affirmation)

Tasting Of Four Elements

Candle Ceremony

Exchange Of Vows

Affirmation Of Vows by the Congregation

Talisman of the Princess

Wrapping of Hands

Jumping of the Broom

Benediction

The Marriage Ceremony

(El Akbur Mishfut The Grand Ceremony)

The pouring of libations

Purpose: The pouring of libations is a long-standing tradition born of the knowledge that life never dies. In our cultures, the libation serves several purposes. It calls on ancestral spirits, divinities, nature, and The Great Spirit to take part in the ceremony. It asks their blessing and guidance on behalf of the couple. It invokes ancestors to complete the circle that links a couple to the cycles of nature, to the unborn and the ones that have passed on to the other side. The Guale/Yamassee philosophy requires that every celebration must invite the entire family to celebrate – to join hands with the past, present, and future.

Ceremony begins with the Official reading the following:

Master Matthew:

"And He Said Unto Them, Have Ye Not Read, That He Which Made Them At The Beginning Made Them Male And Female, And Said, To This Case Should A Man Leave His Father And Mother And Cleve Unto His Wife: And They Twain Should Be

One Flesh. Wherefore They Should No More Twain, But One Flesh. What Therefore The Great Spirit Has Joined Together Let No One Put Asunder."

Master Mustafa: Verse of The Throne

The Giver of Breath (The Most High) is He and without Him, nothing would exist, The Living, The Eternal, who never tires nor takes a second from His creation to slumber or to sleep. For Him is whatever is in the Galactic Heavens and in the planet Earth. Who is he that can intercede with Him except by His permission? He knows what is between their hands (what works their hands do) and what they leave behind; but they cannot comprehend anything from His knowledge except what He pleases. Spread wide is His Seat in the Galactic Heavens and the planet Earth, and the Guardianship of Both of Then is no burden for Him Because He is the Most High, the Supreme."

Consent to Marriage

To The Groom... *Do You Consent To Be Her Husband Before The Eyes Of The Giver of Breath ?*

Groom 3 times   ... *In The Name Of The Giver of Breath , I consent.*

To The Bride... *Do You Consent To Be His Wife Before The Eyes Of The Giver of Breath*

Bride 3 times... *In The Name Of The Giver of Breath , I consent.*

Tasting Of The Four Elements

This ritual dramatizes the "traditional" promise to love "for better or worse, for richer or poorer, in sickness and in health." Four elements: **lemon, vinegar, cayenne pepper,** and **honey** represent the sour, the bitter, the hot, and the sweet times of marriage.

Place each in a crystal bowl which the Official, then positions to correspond to the four directions. Four is also; the number associated with the base of our Native American mounds, as well as the Egyptian pyramid, a symbol of a strong foundation. He then has the couple taste each, beginning with the lemon, and states the following after consumption of each item:

(The Lemon) *I Let Them Know That Marriage Involves Individual Sacrifice, So That Two People Can Harmonize As One;*

(The Vinegar) *But Sacrifice Can Cause bitter Feelings And Bitterness*

(The Cayenne) *Eventually A Heated Explosion*

When The Couple Tastes The Pepper, They Are Cooking, Their Eyes Are Watering ... And The Guests Are Having A Good Time Watching.

(The Honey) But Then He Says... *That If They Can Weather All Of This, All The Difficult Times, And Still Be Friends And Lovers, You Will Come To Understand The Sweetness That is In All The Difficulties of The Previous Three Flavors.*

The Official says: Give Me Your Attention Please.

The Official has the audience to answer: You Have Our Attention

Official- *Oh, Most High, the Great Spirit Who Created The Heavens And The Earth Who Makes the Sun Rise And The World Go Around. To The Creator Of All Things, We lift Our Voices To You. This Ceremony Is In Your Honor And In Honor Of Our Ancestors Who Have Lived And Died Before Us, Grandfathers*

Imani (Faith) To believe with all our heart in our people, our parents our teachers, our leaders, and the righteousness and victory of our struggle.

Vows written by the Bride And Groom.
Optional

I Will Promise Thoughtfulness...

I Will Promise Faithfulness...

I Will Dedicate All My Smiles, Joys And Successes To You...

I Will Commit Tears For Your Sorrows And Pains...

Yet, I Will Have The Strength... And Stamina To See Us Through

Let Me Be Your Shelter

Let Me Comfort You

Think Of My Bosoms As Your Home...

I Promise Be Loyal, Dedicated And Humble....For The Sake Of Our Families... Give You My Love....Second... To Only One .... The Most High.... Which Made This Sacred Union Possible!!!!

Family And Friends...I Asked You All To Come And Witness That On This Day April __,__   I Married My Friend!!!!! My Lover And Yes! My Friend!!!

The Most High Sent You To Me And With Its Gift. I Will Love You For Always And Respect You Throughout Eternity.

Talisman Of The Bride

Official says: The Bride Will Walk Around The Groom Seven Times. This Is An Old Protective Practice Used To Prevent The Malicious Attempts Of Any Disagreeable Spirit Who Is Jealous Of The Happiness Of The Bride And Groom.

Bride: Bride will walk around the groom clockwise seven times.

Consent to Marriage

To The Groom… *Do You Consent To Be Her Husband Before The Eyes Of The Great Spirit?*

Groom 3 times… *In The Name Of The Giver of Breath , I consent.*

To The Bride… *Do You Consent To Be His Wife Before The Eyes Of The Giver of Breath*

Bride 3 times… *In The Name Of The Giver of Breath , I consent.*

The Wrapping of the Hands

(Bring together the right hands of the Groom and the right hand of the Bride. The hands are wrapped in a white shawl. The groom puts the ring on the bride; and the bride puts the ring on the groom:

Groom... *"Behold, thou art consecrated (sacred) Unto Me By This Ring According To The Customs Of MBC/INAAN*

Bride... *"Blessed Are You Oh Sustainers Who Makes The Bridegroom To Rejoice With The Bride."*

OFFICIAL:

"Oh, Make These Loved Companions Greatly To Rejoice, Even As Old, Thou Didst Gladden Thy Creature In The Garden, Blessed Art Thou Oh Sustainer Who Makes Bridegroom And Bride Rejoice."

We Have Been Privileged To Witness A Special Event In The Lives Of This Couple, In The Lives Of this BRIDE and GROOM. They Have Made Their Covenant In Our Presence And Indicated Their Intention To Move Through Life Together. We Are Now Given The Opportunity To Indicate Our Support Of Their Decision.

OFFICIAL: *Do you-all as a congregation, commit yourselves to providing all of the encouragement and support possible to help them in their marriage? If you do, please respond by saying we do.*

The Congregation says: We Do

OFFICIAL: *And Do You-all Agree To Do All In Your Power To Assist Them In The Struggles That They May Encounter? If You Do, Please Respond By Saying, We Do*

The Congregation says: We Do

OFFICIAL: *And Do You-all Give Yourselves To The Ideal Of Living Out A Life Of Commitment That They May See In You That Toward Which They Too Should Strive?*

Congregation: We Do

Official: To Success

May You Live As Long As You Want And Want Nothing As Long As You Live.

If You Have Much, Give From Your Wealth;

If You Have Little, Give From Your Heart.

Jumping the Broom-

The Official shall say: This is done in honor of times when our people *were not allowed* to have official marriage ceremonies in this land. Oh, Great Spirit, this couple willingly gives their minds, hearts, and souls to you as well as each other we ask that you bless this union right now and from this day forward. May their paths always indeed, lead them to one another. With these vows to each other, may their family and friends witness and rejoice and aid them in any time of need. This broom is symbolic of sweeping away any disagreeableness in this place and from this sacred union as well as to sweep away the errors of the past and having a fresh new beginning starting with today.

Oh, Great Spirit and All His Angelic Beings, I Commend Her and Him and Their Offspring Into Your Protection From All Evil.

We seek Refuge in The Giver of Breath's Words, From Every Evil, and The Evil of Every Malicious Eye.

Bride and Groom: Proceed to jump over broom.

Marital Pronouncement!!!

Official: *Now In The Presence of And By The Power Of The Great Spirit (Giver of Breath), And In The Presence Of This Gathering, By The Power Vested In Me By The Indigenous Native*

American Association of Nations Government, I Pronounce You Husband And Wife.

"Oh, Make These Loved Companions Greatly To Rejoice, Even As Old, Thou Didst Gladden Thy Creature In The Garden, Blessed Art Thou Oh Sustainer Who Makes Bridegroom And Bride Rejoice.

A Ceremony for Dedicating Land and Home

The Ceremony for Dedicating Land and Other Possessions Traditionally the ceremony is performed by the Matrun reciting a prayer four times, facing the four directions following of the direction of "The Guale-Yamassee Wheel of Life". The Sweet Grass and/or Smudging Ceremonies begins when the Sweet Grass, incense, or other aromatic is lit.

First, the Sweet Grass, incense, or other aromatic is offered to the Creator, then to the Spirit Keeper of the East, then the South, West, and North. It is offered to Mother Earth and finally to Father Sky. After the area has been cleansed each individual present is then smudged. Each person is to fan the Sweet Grass smoke first to their heart, second to their mind, third around their body and lastly return the smoke to their heart. Sweet Grass is a sacred herb which has the property to bring the positive energies of love. A Sweet Grass Ceremony is a cleansing, purification, and healing process. The Ceremony serves as an opening for prayer circles, gatherings, and other higher ceremonies. The Sweet Grass Ceremony is over when all the people have been smudged. Once the area has been cleansed a sacred place now exists for any events to follow.

The Indigenous Native American Association of Nations' tradition expects this: "It is necessary to return to the rituals of the Earth and invoke the galactic powers that they might come to our aid and put an end to this chaos. He tells us that it is the time for the sixth sun, the sun of unification and solidarity, a sun that will place us in perpendicular communication between earth and sky, and will also balance (bind) the four corners of the Earth, united by the central point that is determined by each human ..."
Lord of the Voice

Matrun or person officiating ceremony recites:

TO THE EAST

Oh, Giver Of Breath Oh, Heavenly Parents Oh, Ancient Ones We Dedicate This Land And Our Home To Your Honor. To The Honor Of All Of Those Before Us We Stand Before Your Great Assembly. Bless The Minds, The Hands, And The Hearts Of

Those Who, Their Works Lead Us To This Destiny. Protect This Land And Our Home From The East. Protect This Land From Enemies Among Us. May This Land Be A Shining Star For Our Clan.

To the South

Oh, Giver Of Breath Oh, Heavenly Parents Oh, Ancient Ones We Dedicate This Land And Our Home To Your Honor. To The Honor Of All Of Those Before Us We Stand Before Your Great Assembly. Bless The Minds, The Hands, And The Hearts Of Those Who, Their Works Lead Us To This Destiny. Protect This Land And Our Home From The South. Protect This Land From Enemies Among Us. May This Land Be A Shining Star For Our Clan.

To the West

Oh, Giver Of Breath Oh, Heavenly Parents Oh, Ancient Ones We Dedicate This Land And Our Home To Your Honor. To The Honor Of All Of Those Before Us We Stand Before Your Great Assembly. Bless The Minds, The Hands, And The Hearts Of Those Who, Their Works Lead Us To This Destiny. Protect This Land And Our Home From The West. Protect This Land From

Enemies Within Us. May This Land Be A Shining Star For Our Clan.

To the North

Oh, Giver Of Breath Oh, Heavenly Parents Oh, Ancient Ones We Dedicate This Land And Our Home To Your Honor. To The Honor Of All Of Those Before Us We Stand Before Your Great Assembly. Bless The Minds, The Hands, And The Hearts Of Those Who, Their Works Lead Us To This Destiny. Protect This Land And Our Home From The North. Protect This Land From Enemies Within Us. May This Land Be A Shining Star For Our Clan.

A Sweet Grass or Smudging Ceremony

A Sweet Grass or Smudging Ceremony

The four sacred plants (Sweet Grass, Tobacco, Cedar and Sage) are mixed equally together to form a sacred smudge used in the sweet grass purification ceremony.

Sweet Grass: Represents kindness and is burned to allow good spirits to enter.

Tobacco: Is used for giving thanks. It is offered to Elders in exchange for advice and information. It is also offered to the Drum Keeper as an offering.

Cedar: Is from the tree of life and is burned to drive out negative forces.

Sage: Is viewed as a women's medicine and offers strength, wisdom, and clarity of purpose. It is symbolic of the life giving powers of women.

The Medicine Wheel represents the wheel of life. The cross in the center of the medicine wheel represents the four directions, the four colors of man (red, black, white, and yellow), and the four seasons. The medicine pouch in the center contains the four sacred medicines (sweet grass, sage, tobacco, and cedar) there are various types of sweet grass. The medicine wheel teaches balance, harmony, and the brotherhood of man.

A Sweet Grass or Smudging Ceremony begins when the Sweet Grass or Smudge is lit.

First the Sweet Grass is offered to the Creator, then to the Spirit Keeper of the East, then the South, West, and North. It is offered to Mother Earth and finally to Father Sky. After the area has been cleansed each individual present is then smudged. Each person is to fan the Sweet Grass smoke first to their heart, second to their mind, third around their body and lastly return the smoke to their heart. Sweet Grass is a sacred herb which has the property to bring the positive energies of love. A Sweet Grass Ceremony is a cleansing, purification, and healing process. The Ceremony serves as an opening for prayer circles, gatherings, and other higher ceremonies. The Sweet Grass Ceremony is over when all the people have been smudged. Once the area has been cleansed a sacred place now exists for any events to follow.

The Mund Bareefan Shagruth Gabelu
Indigenous Native American
Association of Nations Annual
Fire-Rock Eagle
Memorial Commemoration Ceremony
for INAAN Nationals

Over the centuries, Indigenous peoples have embraced many traditions of preparing the remains of their deceased; and many ways of burying their deceased. We shall submit to the traditions of the family of the deceased.

At this time, the family shall have been presented the memorial style of their choice to the person(s) overseeing/servicing the family with the arrangements

With no objections from the family, we suggest the following as a template for the memorial services; and from the services at the burial site.

MEMORIAL SERVICE:

Indigenous music and words from The Prophet- by Kahlil Gibran

The official Shaman/a Clan Mother /or a Chief shall open for the memorial service saying:

Then Almitra spoke, saying, "We would ask now of Death."

And he said:

You would know the secret of death…

But how should you find it unless you seek it in the heart of life?

The owl whose night-bound eyes are blind unto the day cannot unveil the mystery of light.

If you would indeed behold the spirit of death, open your heart wide unto the body of life.

For life and death is one; even as the river and the sea is one.

In the depth of your hopes and desires lies your silent knowledge of the beyond;

And like seeds dreaming beneath the snow your heart dreams of spring.

Trust the dreams, for in them is hidden the gate to eternity.

Your fear of death is but the trembling of the shepherd when he stands before the king whose hand is to be laid upon him in honor.

Is the shepherd not joyful beneath his trembling, that he shall wear the mark of the king?

Yet is he not more mindful of his trembling?

For what is it to die but to stand naked in the wind and to melt into the sun?

And what is to cease breathing, but to free the breath from its restless tides, that it may rise and expand and seek The Great Spirit unencumbered?

Only when you drink from the river of silence shall you indeed sing.

And when you have reached the mountain top, then you shall you begin to climb.

And when the earth shall claim your limbs, then shall you truly dance.

Official says: *There is no time when we consider our "spirit beings" more than at the times of birth and death. When a child is born, we pray for the protection of The Giver of Breath over the sprit coming toward life amongst us from the Giver of Breath . Now we pray that The Most High, The Giver of Breath will hear us again during this time of death.*

A "Clan Chief" should stand before the fire and say:

"The essence of Humans is fashioned in the image of the INVISIBLE Giver of Breath , born before all creatures". That

means you are part of that which created the celestial and terrestrial Universe, the visible thing, and the invisible thing.

It means that the Giver of Breath is the pattern or beginning; and the end or completion of the Created Universe. "The One" is before everything and the Universe has in him, its consistency ahud. Ahud Is Yamassic for: one Love, one Respect, and one Justice.

Chief continues:

A FAMILY PRAYER

The Creative forces of the universe made us a family. We need one another. We love one another. We forgive one another. We work together. We play together. We worship together. Together we use guidance from the ancient ones. Together we grow in memory of our ancestors. Together we love all humans. Together we serve The Giver of Breath. Together we build for paradise. These are our hopes and thoughts. Help us to attain them, O Giver of Breath. In our names and the names of Our Ancestors. This can be trusted.

HOLD ON

Hold on to what is good even if it is a handful of earth.

Hold on to your faith even if it is a tree which stands by itself.

Hold on to what you must do even if it is a long way from here.

Hold on to life even when it is easier letting go.

Hold on to my hand even when I have gone away from you

Traditional

The family and friends may send blessings:

The family and friends may send blessings to the deceased through the ethers of the sacred smoke of the ancestral fire ceremony. Offerings may be silent or verbal.

Words of memory from friends to the family:

_____

_____

_____

_____

_____

At the Burial or Dedication Site:

If possible, this should be spoken in dialect and translated to the assembly on Behalf of the Deceased....

The following prayers are optional and may be replaced by the family and others chosen on behalf of the deceased:

Recitation of Life "The Southern Culture"

We are kin to the ethers, the fire, the air, wind, the water, and the earth.

We are conceived within the cycles of time within this Universe.

With the turn of time, we spring forth, brought through by the nature of and for this planet.

Our essence is shared among many, growing from the branches of a great tree that sprang forth from this land.

Our branches extend, and our foliage continues to spread like a canopy across this Land now called America.

We are called "The Southern Cult." We are indigenous.

Our Heroes

In the story of our villages, our heroes/champions were not individuals who raised up with a history which remained written in the past.

The heroes in our tradition were those who (they) gave their lives with efforts to reach the objectives of history, written as the future by the ancients, building for generations that would follow the steps.

And they were dedicated to that history that was forthcoming - the history of the clans and tribes. Dedicated to the future that was already written. The future and history were united with the life to come and with the dead past which was already gone.

All Stand

Recitation of the Deceased
I/We Give You This One Thought

I/we give you this one thought to keep. I am /We are with you still – I/We do not sleep. I/We are the thousand winds that blow, I am /We are the diamond glints on snow, We are the sunlight on ripened grain, I am /We are the gentle autumn rain. When you awaken in the morning's hush, I am /We are the swift, uplifting rush of quiet birds in circled flight. I am /We are the soft stars that shine at night. Do not think of me/us as gone – I am /We are with you still – in each new dawn.

Prayers, Thoughts and Remembrances of MBC/INAAN

A Poem to My People.

It comes from

"Rufus featuring Chaka Khan"

"I look in your eyes and I can see you've loved so dangerously; You're not trusting your heart(s) to anyone. You tell me you're going to play it smart. We're through before we start. But I believe, we've only just begun ..."

Taino Prayer of Togetherness Among Each Other

Oh, Holy Creator

We thank you for bringing us together. We Thank you for the ancestral and family ties that brings us here as one Pour your spirit on us so that we are no longer separated by our different paths But let us meet and live united on one road of love Let us no longer persecute each other. Let us no longer be persecuted by the negative elements from without and from within Rather lift our spirits into one light, one sound, one song that vibrates and is heard and felt throughout the universe and beyond as it once was, Let this prayer and our peaceful presence be a blessing that gives rest not only to ourselves, but let it bring rest to those that came before us and for those souls yet to be born. Let us be an offering and a prayer to each other.

Heketi Ara Heketi Guaniopia Heketi Yohono.

One people. One Noble spirit. One sweet family.

AHO!

by Jose Tureycu Lopez Yaya Guaili Tribe Cacike Tureycu

This is My Prayer

Oh, Giver of breath, oh creative forces of the galactic universe.

This is my prayer. Give me the strength to continue with this work.

I am lonesome with my pain; my time is running out, but I work. Sometimes I am fragile. Give me the strength, the wisdom, and the patience to prepare the path well that they can carry the job on.   For thousands of years, we have awaited for this time. For this time, I am so grateful to have been chosen as your helper, and I will carry on.

This can be trusted.

(Black-Hawk H. Thunderbird)

Our Heroes

In the story of our villages, our heroes/champions were not individuals who raised up with a history which remained written in the past.

The heroes in our tradition were those who (they) gave their lives with efforts to reach the objectives of history, written as the future by the ancients, building for generations that would follow the steps.

And they were dedicated to that history that was forthcoming - the history of the clans and tribes. Dedicated to the future that was already written. The future and history were united with the life to come and with the dead past which was already gone

Popocatizin

Native American Prayer

Oh, Great Spirit,

Whose voice I hear in the Winds, And whose breath gives life to the world, Hear Me! I am small and weak. I need your strength and wisdom. Let me walk in beauty, and make my eyes ever behold the red and purple sunset.

Make my hands respect the things you have made and my ears sharp to hear your voice. Make me wise so that I may understand the things you have taught my people.

Let me learn the lessons you have hidden in every leaf and rock. I seek strength, not to be greater than my brother, but to fight my greatest enemy- myself.

Make me always ready to come to you with clean hands and straight eyes. So, when lie fades, as the fading sunset, my spirit may come to you without shame.

Life "The Southern Culture"

We are kin to the ethers, the fire, the air, the wind, the water, and the earth.

We are conceived within the cycles of time within this Universe.

With the turn of time, we spring forth, brought through by the nature of and for this planet.

Our essence is shared among many, growing from the branches of a great tree that sprang forth from this land.

Our branches extend, and our foliage continues to spread like a canopy across this Land now called America.

We are called "The Southern Cult." We are indigenous.

B-H Thunderbird

A Family Prayer

The Creative forces of the universe made us a family

We need one another

We love one another

We forgive one another

We work together

We play together We worship together

Together we use guidance from the ancient ones

Together we grow in memory of our ancestor

Together we love all humans

Together we serve The Giver of Breath

Together we build for paradise

These are our hopes and thoughts

Help us to attain them, O Giver of Breath,

In our names and the names of Our Ancestors

This can be trusted.   Traditional

A verse from Master Mustafa

The Giver of Breath does not place upon a person burdens greater than their ability to carry. For it is what it produces, and it is what it earns.

Oh, our Creator, don't punish us when we forget or when we make a mistake. Our Creator don't place on us burdens as you placed on those before us. Our Creator don't place on us what we don't have the ability to carry. Forgive us and grant us protection. Have mercy on us. You are our Creator so grant us help (aid) over the concealers of truth.

"Master Mustafa"

Path of Life Together

I will draw thorns from your feet.

We will walk the path of life together.

Like a brother of my blood.

I will love you.

I will wipe tears from your eyes.

When you are sad,

I will put your aching heart to rest.

Traditional

If You Said

If you said you love the ancient ones, then why don't you trust them? And if you are saying that you have trust in them,

Then I ask you, Why don't you turn to them?

For it is the heavenly ones that are trustworthy.

If you say that you love them, why don't you strive toward them, and if you say you are sensible,

Then I ask you, Why don't you tremble at the mention of the heavenly ones? Surely you all are the etheric parents of us all.

Surely, they birth me. Surely, they provide life and everything for me.

Chief Black TH. Eagle

Hear Me

Hear me four quarters of the world, I am a relative! Give me the strength to walk the Earth.

Give me the eyes to see and the intellect to inner-stand, that I may be like you.

I can face the winds, but only with Your power.

Great Spirit, the faces of all living things are the same all over the earth.

With tenderness have these come up out of the ground.

Look upon these faces of children without number and with children in their arms that they may face the winds and walk the good road to the day of quiet.

This is my prayer, hear me!

Traditional

Hold On

Hold on to what is good even if it is a handful of earth.

Hold on to your faith even if it is a tree which stands by itself.

Hold on to what you must do even if it is a long way from here. Hold on to life even when it is easier letting go. Hold on to my hand even when I have gone away from you.

Traditional

Prayer for Peace

Oh, Supreme Spirit of our Ancestors, I raise my pipe to you. Oh, Supreme Spirit of our Ancestors, to your messengers the four winds; and to Mother Earth who provides for your children

Give us the wisdom to teach our children to love, to respect, and to be kind to each other so that they may grow with peace of mind. Let us learn to share all good things that are of this Earth that you provide for us.

Traditional

Prayer of the Aiders

Oh, Heavenly Ones Who Are Our Sustainers, We Do Accept The Duty That You Have Lain Upon Us; To Recover From The Trials of Our Past…

Oh, Giver of Breath, Our Sustainer. We Beseech You To Keep Your Hand Over Us, To Control The Strings Of The Courses Of Our Lives; Our Sustainer. And If We Do Wrong, Please Shower Your Divine Blessings And Forgiveness On Us, You Are The Only One That Can Raise Us As True Followers Of Truth, And In Your Name We Will Always Carry On.

Remember the Source

When the Supreme Female was worshiped and freely expressed, people of the earth lived in harmony with each other, Nature, and with the Divine. Today, when indigenous people gather our collective energies in ceremony, we open the feminine energy that has been asleep. We activate the Divine Feminine Goddess, "Earth." Today, we honor The Most Principal Matrun Red Silver-Fox Thunderbird, and the Grand Matriarchs of our Clan. It is my pleasure to have the honor to present these very important people to the Clan Mothers and Daughters; Fathers and Sons of our Clan. The Feminine power must share in creation, and give birth over, and over, and over again.

Traditional

I Give You This One Thought

I give you this one thought to keep, I am with you still – I do not sleep. I am a thousand winds that blow, I am the diamond glints on snow, I am the sunlight on ripened grain,
I am the gentle autumn rain.

When you awaken in the morning's hush, I am the swift, uplifting rush of quiet birds in circled flight. I am the soft stars that shine at night. Do not think of me as gone – I am with you still – in each new dawn.
Traditional

The Warm Winds

May the warm winds of heaven blow gently on your house, and may the great spirit bless all who enter. May your moccasins make happy tracks in many snows, and may the rainbow always touch your shoulder.

Navajo Prayer

Now I walk in beauty,

beauty is before me,

beauty is behind me,

above and below me.

Traditional

Great Spirit Prayer

"Oh, Great Spirit, whose voice I hear in the wind, whose breath gives life to all the world. Hear me; I need your strength and wisdom.

Let me walk in beauty, and make my eyes ever behold the red and purple sunset. Make my hands respect the things you have made and my ears sharp to hear your voice. Make me wise so that I may understand the things you have taught my people.

Help me to remain calm and strong in the face of all that comes towards me. Let me learn the lessons you have hidden
in every leaf and rock. Help me seek pure thoughts and act
with the intention of helping others. Help me find compassion without empathy overwhelming me.

I seek strength, not to be greater than my brother, but to fight my greatest enemy, Myself. Make me always ready to come to you with clean hands and straight eyes. So, when life fades, as the fading sunset, my spirit may come to you without shame.

Traditional

A Prayer for Healing

Mother sing me a song that will ease my pain. Mend broken bones. Bring wholeness again. Catch my babies when they are born, Sing my death song. Teach me how to mourn. Show me the Medicine Of the healing herbs, the value of spirit, the way I can serve. Mother heal my heart so that I can see the gifts of yours that can live through me.

Traditional

Sioux Indian Prayer

Hear me, four quarters of the world– a relative I am!

Give me the strength to walk the soft earth.

Give me the eyes to see and the strength to understand,

that I may be like you.

With your power only can I face the winds. Great Spirit…

all over the earth the faces of living things are all alike.

With tenderness have these come up out of the ground.

Look upon these faces of children without number

and with children in their arms,

that they may face the winds and walk the good road

to the day of quiet.

This is my prayer' hear me!

Traditional

The First Dance About The Source

In My Quest To Be A Being, That Is One With You In Perfection And Love, I Come To The Source "The Giver of Breath", And Greet Him With A True And Loving Heart, And I Know that He Loves Me.

He Is The One That Has United Us With All Of You, The Supreme Spirits. The Best One, Oh Guardians, Those Who Form The Circle Of The Master-The Spirit Of Guidance,

We Are One Unit; We are In All. All Is Us; All Is Going To Help Us. All Loves Us. We Are One With You. Oh, Ancients, Elders, Accept Us, Accept Us, Amun. Oh, Ancients, Elders, Accept Us, Accept Us, Amun.

Traditional

Mother Earth Prayer

Mother Earth, hear your child, as I sit here on your lap of grass,

I listen to the quality of your voice in my brother, the wind,

As he blows from all corners and directions.

The soft and gentle raindrops are the tears you cry for your children

Teach me the lessons you offer: to nurture my children as you nurture yours,

To learn the lessons of the Four Kingdoms that make up this world of physical things, and to learn to walk the path chosen so long ago.

Mother Earth hear your child. Be a bond between the worlds of Earth and Spirit.

Let the winds repeat the knowledge of the grandfathers

Who await unseen, yet visible if I only turn my eyes to their world.

Let me hear their voices in the winds that blow to the east.

Let me hear their voices in the winds that blow to the south.

Let me hear their voices in the winds that blow to the west.

Let me hear their voices in the winds that blow to the north.

Traditional

Thank You Prayer

We return thanks to our Mother Earth, who sustains us.

We return thanks to the rivers and streams that supply us with water.

We return thanks to all herbs that furnish medicines for the cure of our diseases.

We return thanks to the moon and stars, which gives us their light when the sun is unseen.

We return thanks to the sun that has looked upon the earth with a generous eye.

Lastly, we return thanks to the Great Spirit who symbolizes all goodness, and who directs all things for the good of his children.
Traditional

To Success

May You Live As Long As You Want And Want Nothing As Long As You Live.

If You Have Much, Give From Your Wealth;

If You Have Little, Give From Your Heart.

Traditional

The (MBC/INAAN) Yamassee medicine pouch contains four sacred medicines (sweet grass, sage, tobacco and cedar) and sabia crystals. The pouch is made of buck skin. The pouch with the crystals represents balance, harmony and the union of humans with nature; and the cycle of life.

Sabia crystals:

The source of the sabia crystals is a certain type of rose According to Guale/Yamassee tradition the rose was buried until the crystals formed. Then, they were placed into the pouch along with red paint to be used for certain occasions like hunting or war. The medicine wheel and the medicine pouch with sabia are closely related in significance and both are present in most Guale/Yamassee ceremonies.

The Snake Stomp Dance

After meeting and dancing, the people would gather sitting in the dance house and make a pictograph of his/her wishes for the upcoming year. A medicine man or shaman would come into the house and show each person's pictographs to the snake one by one over the head of each person. Then, the shaman would take the snake out and let it loose into the forest to carry the wishes into the animal world. This is done because the animals are spirit guides.

The Shadow Knife Stomp Dance

Boys are many sometimes called "ticibane" in our Guale/Yamassee culture. During the coming of age ceremony, or at a naming ceremony, when a ticibane is coming into manhood or declaring his Native American name, he will be given a dagger. Ancient Guale/Yamassee allegedly records this event like this:

When a boy became of age, an elder male relative of importance would make him a knife of this sort from bone and paint it indigo blue. The knife would be buried for thirteen cycles of the moon. Then, by the time it would be dug up, the blue paint would have turned black. The knife would be kept by the boy his entire life, and he would carry it, along with his medicines, on war expeditions. As the time of the man's death, his bundle and his knife were buried with him so that he could use it on his journey to the afterworld.

Another aspect of Proto Yamassee life was focused on the philosophical hero named Ocasta. Below is the legend of Ocasta:

"Yamassee philosophy and religion focused on a culture hero named of Ocasta. Ocasta was one of The Great Spirit's helpers and he was a powerful giant. When he came to earth, he observed people killing animals with flint points. This frightened him so he picked up pieces of flint and made a stone coat to protect himself from humans. Ocasta's only magical power was the ability to disappear but he could not do so in front of human beings. Legend claims that Ocasta was the source of evil. He made witches and other bad things and also traveled from village to village causing trouble. The people disliked his behavior and consequently devised a plan to get rid of him.

They stationed seven nude, "moon-sick" (menstruating) women in the woods where Ocasta would pass. As he came down the path, Ocasta became very ill from seeing so many "moon-sick" women. When he fell down, the women picked some flint from his armor, and then drove a stake into his heart to hold him down. All the men quickly gathered around Ocasta, and he promised to leave earth. Before leaving, however, Ocasta taught the people songs and dances to please the creator and to help them win wars and heal the sick. He had created both good and evil and had sacrificed himself to save the people from the evil he had made. Thus, the story chronicles the origin of good and evil and the gift of medicines to treat evil. One of the most important ceremonies was the Snake Dance. Members of the group assembled in a common area and after a period of dancing, they sat around the dance house. A medicine man would then appear carrying a poisonous snake. Each person would draw a small pictograph on a piece of bark representing his wishes for the year. Then the medicine man would walk slowly around the circle holding the snake's head so that it could see the pictographs. He would then release the snake in the woods to carry Yamassee wished into the animal world".

This was a story told to make children behave. "If you don't be good, Ocasta is going to get you". We do not do this anymore.

Thank you

Made in the USA
Monee, IL
04 May 2021